STEAM PORTFOLIOS 7

SOUTH EASTERN STEAM

Rodney Lissenden

First published 1991

ISBN 0 7110 1956 8

© Ian Allan Ltd 1991

Published by

IAN ALLAN LTD

Terminal House Shepperton TW17 8AS
Telephone: Walton-on-Thames (0932) 228950
Fax: 0932 232366   Telex: 929806 IALLAN G
Registered Office: Terminal House Shepperton TW17 8AS
Phototypeset and Printed by Ian Allan Printing at their works at Coombelands in Runnymede, England

Front cover: 'Battle of Britain' class 4-6-2 No 34085 *502 Squadron* approaches Petts Wood Junction with the down 'Golden Arrow' on 16 May 1958. The appearance of the train was somewhat spoilt by the addition of British Railways Mk 1 coaches to the formation. As can be seen from the clean ballast, the track layout had been extensively altered and realigned. The previous track-bed can be seen curving away behind the locomotive. *R.C. Riley*

Right: The driver's eye view from the footplate of Brighton 'Terrier' No 32678 at Newhaven depot on 30 July 1963. *Trevor Owen*

INTRODUCTION

The area covered by this book is the South-east area of the Southern Region, now part of Network SouthEast. The origins of the lines in the area lie with the South Eastern Railway and the London, Chatham & Dover Railway. These two companies amalgamated in 1899 to become the South Eastern & Chatham Railway. In addition, a small part of the London, Brighton & South Coast Railway is included within these pages. Most of these photographs are taken to the east of the Brighton main line and span the years between 1952 and 1965.

My interest in railways goes back to the early years of the war when I was lifted to look over a railway bridge on the LCDR main line near Herne Bay and later, after the war, the sight of No 21C1 *Channel Packet* on the 'Golden Arrow' thundering through Beckenham Junction cemented my interest in railways. The Southern was always my first love, with such a variety of locomotives and the memories of summer Saturdays in the early 1950s when Stewarts Lane depot was hard pushed to supply enough locomotives for all the extra trains to the Kent coast resorts. Many freight locomotives were pressed into service, the 'Lane' never let down the passengers!

I have had the privilege of viewing many slides and have selected the most interesting and historic pictures – it has been a most enjoyable yet difficult task. I should like to thank all the photographers who have supplied me with irreplaceable transparencies and for their help and patience in the production of this book. Also thanks are due to the Railway Correspondence & Travel Society for their agreement to the use of all the statistical information taken from the series of Southern Railway locomotive histories written by D.L. Bradley.

Special thanks are due to my daughter Julia for planning the layout of the book. It should be appreciated that many of the slides are old and some have faded slightly, but it was felt that these minor blemishes would not detract from the book.

Rodney Lissenden
Otford, Kent
November 1990

Left: A train of great interest was the 11.50am (Saturdays only) Victoria-Ramsgate, which in the final days of steam on the London-Chatham main line was regularly worked by a rebuilt Wainwright 4-4-0. 'D1' class No 31145 is seen passing Shortlands signalbox, having climbed the 1 in 97 from Ravensbourne on the Catford loop line to regain the main line. The fine signalbox was to disappear a few months after this photograph was taken on 16 May 1959. Note the replacement box on the left-hand side. *R.C.Riley*

Above: A lovely country scene at Hever on 31 May 1963, with 'H' class 0-4-4T No 31543 on an Oxted-Uckfield train. Note the LBSCR oil lamp and the British Railways totem station sign on the right. The building on the left and the station canopy have been swept away, but the station building and the footbridge still survive today. *Trevor Owen*

3

Left: Ex-SECR 'N' class 2-6-0 No 31865 is seen at Folkestone Warren on a Reading-Dover train in 1960. The building of this locomotive was commenced at Woolwich Arsenal and completed at Ashford works in June 1925, with withdrawal taking place in September 1963. The section of line between Folkestone and Dover is one of the most expensive on British Rail today, with the constant threat of rockfall and subsidence being monitored at all times. *Derek Cross*

Right: 'Schools' class 4-4-0 No 30934 *St Lawrence* hurries through Folkestone Warren with a Deal-Charing Cross train in June 1960. On 11 May 1941 as Southern Railway No 934, *St Lawrence* was severely damaged near Cannon Street station. As an air raid by German bombers commenced, No 934 was standing with empty stock at platform 2 when incendiaries set the station roof on fire. The crew with the assistance of 'H' class No 1541 attempted to remove all the rolling stock to safety. Most had been successfully cleared when the two locomotives coupled to five carriages and two electric multiple-units began crossing the bridge over the Thames. Several high-explosive bombs fell nearby, forcing the crew to stop and take cover. This was perhaps just as well as one bomb hit the cab of the 'Schools', piercing the firebox and wrecking the top of the tender. No 934 was soon taken to Eastleigh works for repairs and was returned to traffic on 27 August 1941. *Derek Cross*

Above: William Adams, chief mechanical engineer of the London & South Western Railway between 1878 and 1895, designed the 'T3' class 4-4-0 for use on West of England expresses. No 563, seen at Brighton shed on 13 April 1958 was built at Nine Elms works, being completed in March 1893. A total of 20 members of the class were built, and lasted until the mid-1930s when all but two were withdrawn. No 563 was given a general repair and repaint at Eastleigh works in the autumn of 1935 and lasted through the war, being withdrawn in August 1945. Fortunately No 563 was not broken up, and survived until 1948 when it was overhauled and repainted in 1903 Drummond livery to appear at the Waterloo centenary celebrations. The locomotive was retained after the exhibition and eventually was displayed at the Clapham museum of transport, subsequently moving to the National Railway Museum at York, where it can be seen today. *Trevor Owen*

Below: A fine portrait of ex-LSWR 'T9' class 4-4-0 No 30338, seen outside Brighton works on 15 March 1953 after full overhaul, awaiting the fitting of its smokebox number plate. This locomotive designed by Dugald Drummond was the last of the class to be built at the LSWR's Nine Elms works, and was completed in October 1901. It worked for nearly 60 years, being withdrawn in April 1961 having completed 1,879,273 miles in service. Fortunately one member of the class, No 30120, has been preserved as part of the national collection. *Trevor Owen*

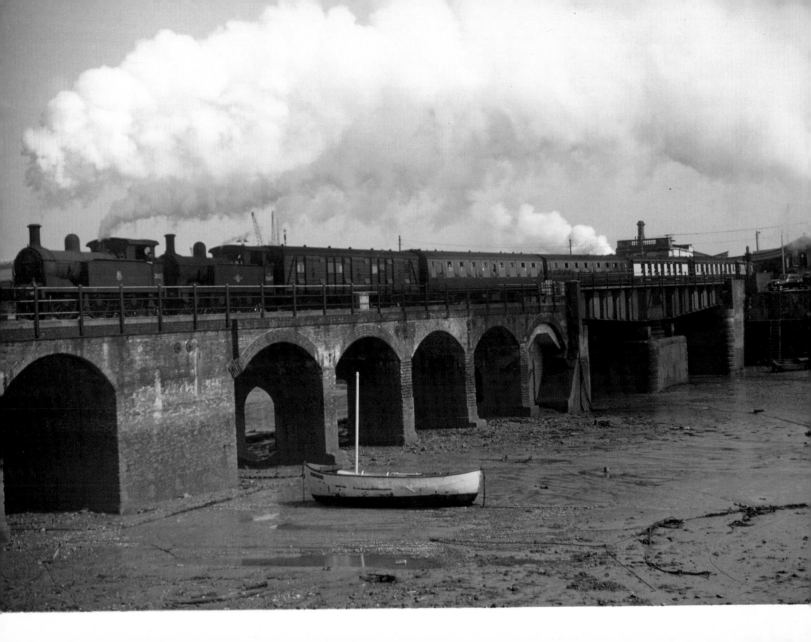

Left: James Stirling would have been proud to see two of his 0-6-0T locomotives storming up the 1 in 30 gradient from Folkestone Harbour to Folkestone Junction with the 'Golden Arrow' approximately 60 years after their construction. 'R1' class Nos 31107 and 31047, built in June 1898 and August 1895 respectively, are probably assisted by a further one or two 'R1' tanks at the rear of the train, as indicated by the smoke visible. The final years of the class were spent at Folkestone Junction shed, with the last being withdrawn in early 1960. Unfortunately none were preserved. *Derek Cross*

Above: Maunsell 'King Arthur' class 4-6-0 No 30806 *Sir Galleron* leaves Cannon Street with the 5.47pm to Pluckley on 5 June 1958. The former Southern Railway No 806 was the last 'King Arthur' to be built, leaving Eastleigh works in January 1927. It was withdrawn from service in April 1961 having completed 1,127,000 miles in traffic. *R.C.Riley*

Left: A very fine view of BR Standard Class 5 4-6-0 No 73081 at St Mary Cray Junction with a Victoria-Ramsgate train in the summer of 1958. The layout in the area of Bickley, Petts Wood and St Mary Junction was redesigned in the late 1950s to facilitate the operation of the new electric service to the Kent coast, and to ease several sharp curves. The author has happy memories of No 73081, having had the privilege of a footplate ride from Victoria to Folkestone Junction. Driver Percy Tutt of Stewarts Lane showed great skill in handling 12 coaches on a boat train to Folkestone Junction via Maidstone East, arriving three minutes early. *Derek Cross*

Above: BR Standard Class 4 2-6-4T No 80085 climbs the 1 in 47 incline out of Tonbridge towards Somerhill tunnel on the 5.12pm to Eastbourne on 7 August 1964. Ex-LMS Fairburn and BR Standard 2-6-4Ts replaced most of the former SECR and LBSCR tank locomotives on the heavier branch line workings during the 1950s. Tonbridge shed was situated behind the last coach of the train. *C.Berridge*

Above: Ex-LBSCR 'E4' class 0-6-2T No 32468 is seen at Brighton shed on 31 March 1962. Designed by R.J.Billinton, this locomotive was built at Brighton works, appearing in May 1898, and was withdrawn in January 1963. There were a total of 75 members of 'E4' Class, all of which were built at Brighton between December 1897 and September 1903. Each member of the class was given a name, No 32468 having formerly been named *Midhurst*. Its final mileage on withdrawal was 1,160,877 miles after an interesting career lasting 65 years. As Southern Railway No 2468 it was shedded at Eastbourne, and on 4 May 1942 was damaged by one of the fighter bomber raids on the South Coast. On 20 May the locomotive was towed to Ashford works for repair, where a live cannon shell was found embedded in the coal bunker, and bomb splinters in the left-hand tank. *Trevor Owen*

Right: Ex-LBSCR 0-6-0T No 82 *Boxhill,* one of William Stroudley's famous 'Terriers' is seen at Brighton shed on 13 April 1958. No 82 was built in August 1880 as a member of Class A1. In 1905 its wheel arrangement was altered to 2-4-0T and trials were run on the Brighton-Worthing motor train; it was returned to the 0-6-0T arrangement in June 1913. In 1920 as No 682 it was lettered Loco Dept Brighton Works and spent many years as works shunter. In 1932 it was returned in the Southern Railway service stock lists as No 380S. By 1946 No 380S was replaced as works shunter by No 2635, which was transferred to service stock as No 377S. The displaced 'A1' was taken into works and returned to the Stroudley livery of 50 years before. As No 82 *Boxhill* it was displayed at the Waterloo centenary celebrations and various other exhibitions until it was moved to store at Tweedmouth shortly after this photograph was taken. The locomotive was taken to Eastleigh works for refurbishment, prior to being sent to Clapham transport museum and later to the National Railway Museum, York. *Trevor Owen*

Above: Graceful ex-SECR 'L' class 4-4-0 No 31768 arrives at Shepherdswell on a stopping train to Dover Priory on 23 May 1959. Designed by H.S.Wainwright as a successor to the successful 'D' and 'E' classes, the 'L' class was built after proposals for a 4-6-0 design were abandoned when this was judged to be too heavy for the Chatham main line. R.E.L.Maunsell replaced Wainwright in January 1914 and the 'L' class design was modified by the Ashford drawing office prior to construction. 12 members of the class were built by Beyer Peacock & Co at a cost of £4,195 each and 10 were built by A.Borsig of Berlin. No 31768 was one of the Manchester-built examples, and was delivered to the SECR in September 1914. It was withdrawn in December 1961 and broken up at Eastleigh works, having covered a total of 1,568,447 miles. *R.C.Riley*

Below: A splendid photograph taken at Ashford shed on 12 September 1954 prior to the final leg of the Railway Correspondence & Travel Society's 'Invicta' railtour from Ashford to Blackfriars via the Crowhurst spur and the Mid-Kent line. 'E' class 4-4-0 No 31166 has its number painted on the front bufferbeam, and the words British Railways in full on the tender, whilst 'D' class 4-4-0 No 31737 is still in beautiful condition a few months after a full overhaul. Both locomotives were designed by H.S.Wainwright of the SECR, with No 31166 being constructed by Kitson of Leeds in 1907, and No 31737 being built at Ashford works in 1906. The 'E' was the last of the class in service, being withdrawn in May 1955, whilst the 'D' was withdrawn in November 1956. Between them the two locomotives covered a grand total of 3,181,212 miles. *Trevor Owen*

Above: Bulleid 'West Country' Pacific No 34091 *Weymouth* leaves Dover Marine with the up 'Golden Arrow' for Victoria on 12 July 1958. The site of Dover motive power depot was behind the locomotive; this is now occupied by sidings for traffic to and from the continent. *Trevor Owen*

Right: The SECR 'H' class 0-4-4T was designed by H.S.Wainwright, and all 66 locomotives were built at Ashford works between 1904 and 1909, except for the final two, which appeared in 1915, at an average cost of £2,380. No 31177 is seen at Hawkhurst, the terminus of the branch from Paddock Wood, on 3 June 1961. *F.Hornby*

Above: No 31069 was originally built as a member of the James Stirling 'R' class for the South Eastern Railway in June 1898, and rebuilt by the SECR to Class R1 in December 1910. Some members of the class retained their Stirling cabs and received stovepipe chimneys and low domes to work the Whitstable Harbour branch; the clearance through Tyler Hill tunnel at Canterbury being very restricted. No 31069 was the only example to have a tall chimney and dome whilst retaining the Stirling cab, and is seen at Ashford shed on 1 June 1958 shortly after withdrawal. *Trevor Owen*

Below: The 'Q' class 0-6-0 locomotives were designed by R.E.L.Maunsell and a total of 20 were ordered from Eastleigh works in March 1936 at a cost of £7,200 each. Before construction commenced, however, ill health caused Maunsell's retirement and it was left to his successor O.V.S.Bulleid to see the class into traffic. The class was numbered 530-549 and entered service between January 1938 and September 1939, being used on a variety of goods and slow passenger services mainly on the Western and Central sections of the Southern, with only occasional visits to the Eastern division. In August 1955 No 30549, seen here at Norwood Junction on 20 May 1960, was fitted with a BR Class 4 blastpipe and a stovepipe chimney, much to the surprise of local officials. Steaming was vastly improved, as were water and coal consumption. At Bournemouth No 30549 was highly regarded, and was usually rostered for Saturday passenger services on the Swanage and Lymington branches. The last of the class was withdrawn in May 1965, with No 30549 having been condemned in July 1963. No 30541 was the only example to be preserved, eventually finding a home on the Bluebell Railway. *R.C.Riley*

Left: 'King Arthur' No 30800 *Sir Meleaus de Lile* tops the 1 in 82 climb out of Whitstable with an excursion bound for Margate and Ramsgate on 7 June 1959. Note the ex-SECR matchboard boat train brake end behind the locomotive. *M.R.Galley*

Right: Ivatt Class 2MT 2-6-2T No 41313 leaves Faversham for Sittingbourne with a local train on 17 April 1959. Former LMS locomotives began to appear in Kent during the latter part of the 1950s, and worked on most secondary passenger duties. *M.R.Galley*

Below: 'H' class 0-4-4T No 31512 stands in the centre road at Gravesend Central awaiting the next duty on the Allhallows branch. The make up of the train is of interest, with an additional coach in red livery of SECR origins having been added to the usual Maunsell push-pull set. The scene has changed considerably since this view was recorded on 24 September 1960. *Trevor Owen*

Left: 'H' class 0-4-4T No 31193 with a Railway Correspondence & Travel Society special at Deptford Wharf on 3 October 1959. The London, Brighton & South Coast Railway opened the branch from New Cross Gate to Deptford Wharf in 1849. It never had a regular passenger service.
Rodney Lissenden

Above: Ramsgate depot on 28 March 1959 with 'King Arthur' No 30793 *Sir Ontzlake* awaiting its next duty for Victoria, and ex-SECR 'D' class 4-4-0 No 31501 minus its leading driving wheel, being used as a stationary steam heating boiler.
R.C.Riley

Left: A location which has changed beyond all recognition since this photograph was taken on 12 July 1958. By the late 1980s this area had become the site of the Channel tunnel works, with the exact spot where the photographer stood being covered with pre-fabricated concrete segments for lining the tunnels. Rebuilt 'West Country' class 4-6-2 No 34013 *Okehampton* passes Shakespeare Cliff signalbox (it is interesting to note that a fire was required in July) with a down train to Ramsgate via Dover. *Trevor Owen*

Right: Bulleid 'Battle of Britain' class Pacific No 34061 *73 Squadron* drifts down the 1 in 95 gradient from Bickley to Bromley South at the head of the 12.10pm boat train from Folkestone Harbour to Victoria via the South Eastern main line through Tonbridge. The very smart EPB unit is on a Victoria-Orpington service. This scene was photographed on 11 June 1961. *B.C.Bending*

Above: 'H' class No 31308 waits to depart from Dunton Green with a Westerham branch train in September 1961, having just taken over from No 31177 of the same class. This and the next two photographs illustrate the Westerham valley branch, which was opened by the South Eastern Railway on 6 July 1881. The line served Brasted, Westerham and the small village of Chevening, which only merited a halt. The total construction cost was about £70,000, and the line was single track throughout, with a passing loop at Brasted. *Roy Hobbs*

Right: The 'H' class tank locomotives worked most of the branches in the south-east. They were very popular with footplate crews, being reliable and free-steaming. No 31518 on Tonbridge shed duty No 239 is seen leaving Brasted for Dunton Green on the last day of operations on the Westerham branch, 28 October 1961. The locomotive was suitably adorned 'Flyer 1881-1961'. For observant motorists travelling west on the M25 motorway, the old station house and coal yard can still be seen between junctions 5 and 6. *J.G.Dewing*

Left: 'H' class No 31512 stands at Westerham on 27 September 1959. The locomotive was built in January 1909 at Ashford works and was converted to motor working in November 1951, enabling it to work push-pull trains on the many branches in the south-east. The station at Westerham has since been demolished and the site covered by a factory estate. *F.Hornby*

Below: A sad picture, recording the final run of the last 'D1' and 'E1' class locomotives en route to Ashford works for scrap, and seen shunting an engineer's train at Bat & Ball sidings, Sevenoaks, in November 1961. 'D1' No 31749 was originally built in 1903 by Vulcan Foundry, was rebuilt by Beyer Peacock in 1921, and covered 1,779,348 miles in 58 years of service. 'E1' No 31067 was built at the Ashford works of the South Eastern & Chatham Railway in 1908, and rebuilt by Beyer Peacock in 1920. Unfortunately no examples of either class survived into preservation. The former Southern Railway bogie brake van seen in this view was built at Ashford in 1936. A number of these bogie brake vans could still be seen at work in Kent on Channel Tunnel construction trains some 55 years later. *R.C.Riley*

Right: Push-pull set No 650, formed of coaches Nos S6940 and S2087 built by the LBSCR in 1921, being propelled by ex-SECR 'H' class 0-4-4T No 31517 on a local train from Tonbridge to Tunbridge Wells West near High Brooms on 20 June 1959. *Rodney Lissenden*

Below: As late as 1 October 1961, former Southern Railway hauled stock coaches could be seen in ex-works condition. Maunsell 59ft corridor brake third No S3705S, part of set No 189 and built in 1931, is seen at New Cross Gate. *Rodney Lissenden*

Above: London Transport Beyer Peacock 0-4-4T No L44 takes water at New Cross Gate, having worked a railtour onto the Southern on 1 October 1961. *Rodney Lissenden*

Right: 'L1' class 4-4-0 No 31754 passes St Mary Cray Junction with a Dover Priory-Victoria train on 14 June 1958. The work to increase the track layout from two lines to four has just begun, with the earthworks visible behind the locomotive. *R.C.Riley*

Below: The final 5.44pm Cannon Street-Ramsgate service sets out from the capital on Friday 12 June 1959, hauled by rebuilt 'West Country' No 34004 *Yeovil*. Obviously some enthusiasts were enjoying the last run prior to electric traction taking over on the following Monday. It is interesting to note that during the 12 months between the photograph on page 9 and that shown here, the overall roof has been removed. Subsequently an office block has been built above the platforms in more modern times. *R.C.Riley*

Above: 'O1' class 0-6-0 No 31258 arrives at Shepherdswell with a Railway Enthusiasts Club special to the East Kent Railway on 23 May 1958. A light freight locomotive built at Ashford works in May 1894, and rebuilt in May 1914, No 31258 was one of the last members of the class to be withdrawn, being condemned in December 1961. Due to their light axle loading, eight of the class were retained until the end of 1961 to work in the Kent coalfield and around the Dover harbour area. *R.C.Riley*

Above: Ex-SECR 'D1' class 4-4-0 No 31739, was built originally as a member of Class D in 1902 at Ashford works and rebuilt as Class D1 in 1927, also at Ashford. The locomotive was withdrawn in November 1961, having covered 2,002,974 miles in 59 years, the highest mileage of any Wainwright 4-4-0. No 31739 is seen at Dunton Green reversing from the down South Eastern main line to gain access to the Westerham branch to work the final day's traffic in conjunction with 'H' class No 31518 and 'Q1' class No 33029 on 28 October 1961. *B.C.Bending*

Below: The perfect lines and livery of a Wainwright 'Coppertop' beautifully preserved by Ashford works, seen on 20 June 1960 outside the shops where it had been built 54 years earlier. Withdrawn as No 31737 in November 1956, the locomotive spent over a year deteriorating outside Ashford works before being transferred to the disused roundhouse at Tweedmouth. By August 1959 preparation for restoration was well advanced and No 31737 was returned to the Southern Region, being taken into Ashford works on 15 December 1959. By May 1960 restoration was complete, and in SECR livery No 737 was taken by road to Clapham Museum, moving subsequently to the National Railway Museum at York. *R.C.Riley*

Left: 'Schools' class No 30925 *Cheltenham* heads towards Clayton tunnel at the head of an RCTS railtour from London Bridge to Brighton on Sunday 7 October 1962. A few weeks earlier on 1 September 1962 No 30925 worked the 10.15 Waterloo-West of England service, reaching Exeter three minutes early with a load of 10 coaches. It returned to Waterloo the following day with the 11am from Exeter. This was an unusual working, and probably the last visit of a 'Schools' to Exeter. The locomotive was withdrawn in December 1962 together with the other final 17 members of the class. It covered 1,127,788 miles during 28 years of service, and has subsequently found a home at the National Railway Museum, York. *Trevor Owen*

Above: Rebuilt 'West Country' Pacific No 34001 *Exeter* passes Weald intermediate signalbox on the climb from Tonbridge to Sevenoaks with a Ramsgate-Charing Cross train in the summer of 1960. The formation of the train is of interest, consisting of two sets of British Railways coaches, one ex-Southern Railway set and one single coach at the rear. The ride in the last coach, known as a 'swinger', was usually interesting to say the least! *Derek Cross*

Above: In June 1959 ex-Southern Railway 'L1' class 4-4-0 No 31789 and 'West Country' class 4-6-2 No 34093 *Saunton* pass Weald signalbox on the six mile climb of 1 in 122 and 1 in 144 between Tonbridge and Sevenoaks. The train, one of the heaviest on the South Eastern section, is the famous 'Night Ferry' overnight sleeper from Paris to London. The weight of the seven Wagon Lits coaches together with the vans and the conventional coaches attached at Dover was well over 500 tons. The 'L1' was built at Ashford works in April 1926 and withdrawn in November 1961, having covered 999,423 miles, whilst *Saunton* was built at Brighton works in October 1949, rebuilt in May 1960 at Eastleigh, and withdrawn in July 1967 after running a total of 888,004 miles. *Derek Cross*

Right: 'Battle of Britain' class 4-6-2 No 34089 *602 Squadron* runs into Sevenoaks with the down 'Golden Arrow' in the spring of 1960. This view from the A2028 road bridge has changed considerably since this photograph was taken. The original South Eastern Railway signalbox was replaced by a modern power box in the early 1960s, which will itself become redundant when the area comes under the control of Ashford. The coal yard on the left now has no rail access, the telegraph poles have disappeared, and the North Downs in the background have been cut through by the M25 motorway. *Derek Cross*

Below: Ex-SECR 'D1' class 4-4-0 No 31247 passes Folkestone Warren at the head of a Victoria-Ramsgate train via Dover Priory in the spring of 1960. The bridge, huts, telegraph poles and station halt have all since been swept away, making this photograph of historical interest. *Derek Cross*

Left: Brighton shed seen on 13 April 1958 from Howard Place. The main line to London can just be seen between the buildings and the splendid 330yd London Road viaduct, which carries the line towards Lewes and Eastbourne on 27 brick arches. The 16-road shed buildings were opened in 1861, the original tiled gabled roofs were replaced by an asbestos roof in 1938 when some roads were left open to the elements. The depot at this time was full of interesting locomotives. Some of those visible include preserved ex-LSWR No 563, Classes H15 and M7, ex-LBSCR 'Terrier',

Classes C2X, E4, K, Standard Class 4, as well as former LSWR and LBSCR departmental coaches. Other locomotives in the shed but not visible in the picture included a Brighton Atlantic, 'King Arthur', 'West Country' and ex-SECR 'L' class. *Trevor Owen*

Above: Ex-LBSCR 'E2' class 0-6-0T No 32100 is seen at Stewarts Lane shed on 1 March 1959. The class of 10 locomotives was designed by L.B.Billinton and built at Brighton works between June 1913 and October 1916. The delay in the construction of such a small class was due to the disruption caused by World War 1. The class saw service in every section of the Southern Railway, working local freight and shunting yards. The last few years in traffic were served in Southampton docks, Dover, Battersea and Herne Hill yards. *R.C.Riley*

41

Right: Ex-SECR 'C' class 0-6-0 No 31256 arrives at Horsomden on an early morning train to Hawkhurst on 11 June 1961, a few days prior to the closure of the branch. *Roy Hobbs*

Below: In 1950 Captain Howey, chairman of the Romney, Hythe & Dymchurch Railway, purchased 0-4-4T *Dunrobin* from the Duke of Sutherland. The locomotive was built in 1895 and spent the next 55 years at Golspie in Sutherland. On 20 March 1950 *Dunrobin* and its saloon coach set off under its own power for Perth and then on to Carlisle. The locomotive and coach were then towed via Leeds, Toton, Wellingborough, Cricklewood and Hither Green to Ashford in easy stages. On arrival at Ashford a week was spent in the works in preparation for the last stage of the journey, again in steam, to New Romney, where the locomotive finally arrived on 28 March after a journey of 745 miles, over half of which had been accomplished under her own steam. The next 15 years were spent at the RH&DR, but unfortunately *Dunrobin* was sold again, and departed for Canada on 11 March 1965, the day on which this photograph was taken. *J.G.Dewing*

Right: An unusual visitor is seen at Norwood Junction depot on 15 September 1963. Former Caledonian Railway 4-2-2 No 123, built by Neilson & Co in 1886 to a Drummond design, had come south to work the 'Blue Belle' railtour to the Bluebell Railway in tandem with ex-LSWR 'T9' class 4-4-0 No 120. No 123 is now housed in the Glasgow Transport Museum, whilst No 120 is part of the national collection. *Rodney Lissenden*

Left: Ex-Southern Railway 'L1' class 4-4-0 No 31782 rolls into Shepherdswell with a train on 23 May 1959 a few weeks before the power was switched on to electrify a large part of north and east Kent. Electrification increased the withdrawal of many steam locomotives as well as fine items of rolling stock such as the Maunsell Hastings-gauge coaches shown here. *Trevor Owen*

Right: BR Standard Class 4 2-6-0 No 76031 leaves Redhill with the 6.53pm to Tonbridge on 30 April 1963. Various BR Standard designs appeared in the south-east during the latter days of steam. *C.Berridge*

Below: Some 122 members of Class O were built by Ashford works and Sharp Stewart for the South Eastern Railway to a design by James Stirling. No 31048, originally numbered 48, was one of those built at Ashford, being completed in December 1893 at a cost of £1,550. It was rebuilt to Class O1 in August 1908. 56 members of the class entered Southern Railway stock in 1923, and 52 Southern Railway examples together with three from the East Kent Railway were absorbed by British Railways in 1948. A large number of these were withdrawn between 1948 and 1951, and only 11 examples actually had 30,000 added to their numbers under the Southern Region numbering scheme. No 31048 is seen at Stewarts Lane depot on 24 May 1958, two and a half years before withdrawal. No 31065 survived to be privately preserved. *R.C.Riley*

Above: James Stirling was responsible for designing the South Eastern Railway 'R' class 0-6-0T, of which the first example to be built was No 335, completed at Ashford works in June 1888 at a cost of £1,280. It was rebuilt and reclassified as Class R1 in March 1915. When new the locomotive was delivered to Hastings shed, and was withdrawn from St Leonards shed in July 1955 having spent 67 years in the same area. It is at its final home of St Leonards that the former No 335 is seen on 15 May 1954 as British Railways No 31335. *Trevor Owen*

Below: The 90 ton 2-6-4T freight locomotives of Class W were an indirect development of the ill-fated 'K' class and the Maunsell 'N1' class 2-6-0 design. No 31924, seen at Hither Green depot on 12 March 1960, was built at Ashford works, being completed in February 1936. It was withdrawn in July 1964 and scrapped by George Cohen of Kettering. Members of the class were used extensively on cross-London freight duties, based at Hither Green and Norwood Junction depots. No 31924 was the first to be transferred to the West Country, where it was used on banking duties between Exeter St Davids and Central stations. On withdrawal it had completed 424,096 miles. *Trevor Owen*

Above: The 'C' class 0-6-0 goods locomotives were designed by H.S.Wainwright for the SECR in 1899, with the first example being completed in 1900. A total of 109 were built between 1900 and 1908, being constructed by the SECR at its Ashford and Longhedge works, together with Neilson, Reid & Co and Sharp Stewart. The total weight of engine and tender in working order was just over 82 tons. These well designed, free-steaming locomotives were to be seen on main-line freight, secondary passenger and excursion duties in the south of England for over 65 years. No 31712, seen at Ashford depot on 12 September 1954, had just received a major works overhaul. Built by Sharp Stewart in 1900, it was withdrawn in February 1957. *Trevor Owen*

49

Left: 'Schools' class 4-4-0 No 30911 *Dover* stands at Cannon Street with the 6.15pm to Folkestone in June 1959. The 'Schools' class was without doubt the finest passenger locomotive designed by Maunsell, and one of the most powerful 4-4-0 designs ever produced. *Dover* was completed at Eastleigh works in December 1932, and withdrawn in December 1962. *A.Endersby*

Right: The first Bulleid Pacific, 'Merchant Navy' class No 35001 *Channel Packet* passes Shorncliffe with an up boat train from Dover Marine to Victoria in June 1959. The two white discs above the buffers denote a train routed via Tonbridge and the South Eastern main line. The 'Merchant Navy' class were the most powerful Southern Railway class, designed by O.V.S.Bulleid and built at Eastleigh works. *Channel Packet* appeared in June 1941, numbered 21C1, being renumbered 35001 in October 1949. Eastleigh works rebuilt the locomotive in August 1959, and it was finally withdrawn in November 1966 having travelled 1,095,884 miles in 23 years. Unfortunately *Channel Packet* did not survive the cutter's torch, but several of the class have been retained for preservation, including No 35028 *Clan Line* which has appeared regularly on British Rail metals, and No 35029 *Ellerman Lines* at the National Railway Museum, York. *Derek Cross*

Above: 'Terrier' No 32678 was built for the
LBSCR as No 78 *Knowle* in 1880, and on
withdrawal in 1963 was sold for static display at
Butlins holiday camp at Minehead. It later passed
to the nearby West Somerset Railway, and thence
to the Kent & East Sussex Railway. No 32678 is
seen on the last working on the West Quay
branch to Newhaven West breakwater on 30 July
1963. *Trevor Owen*

Right: Brighton Atlantic No 32424 *Beachy Head*
with a Railway Correspondence & Travel Society
'Brighton Works Centenary' railtour on 5 October
1952. Douglas Earle Marsh designed these fine
locomotives after arriving from the Great
Northern Railway in 1904. Only 11 examples
were built, the first five being constructed by
Kitson of Leeds as Class H1, and the remaining
six produced by Brighton works in 1911 as Class

H2. No 32424 was the last to be withdrawn,
succumbing in April 1958, having covered
1,090,661 miles in its 47-year working life.
Unfortunately no 'Brighton Atlantic' survives in
preservation, although the Bluebell Railway has a
former GNR Atlantic boiler, which might serve as
the basis of a reproduction of an LBSCR Atlantic.
Trevor Owen

Left: A splendid study of 'King Arthur' No 30767 *Sir Valence* on the down 'Kentish Belle' for Ramsgate about to pass 'N' class 2-6-0 No 31404 at the head of a Victoria-Ramsgate excursion. The heat of the day, which is 5 August 1957, and the exceptionally clean fires of each locomotive belie the fact that the trains are nearly at the summit of the 1 in 95 climb from Bromley South to between the station and junction at Bickley. Note the all-Pullman formation of the 'Kentish Belle' and the plum and spilt milk liveried Hastings gauge stock of the excursion. *R.C.Riley*

Left: 'C' class 0-6-0 No 31692 stands at Hither Green depot on 12 March 1960. This locomotive was built by Neilson, Reid & Co in July 1900 (works No 5698) and withdrawn in April 1960. It is remarkable that 54 of the original 109 members of this class were still in service at the end of 1960, and that 13 received general repairs and repaints at Ashford works during that year. *Trevor Owen*

Below: Ex-SECR 'D1' class 4-4-0 No 31749 in beautiful condition passes Selsdon with a Sussex lines inspection special in August 1961, only three months prior to withdrawal. *Roy Hobbs*

Above: The 'Q1' class 0-6-0 was designed by Bulleid as a heavy goods locomotive for the Southern Railway, with construction being shared between Ashford and Brighton works. The 40 members of the class were originally numbered C1-C40, becoming British Railways Nos 33001-40; all being built during 1942 at a cost of just over £9,000 each. The working life of the class was a mere 24 years, with the highest mileage attained being just over half a million miles. The first member of the class, No 33001, was withdrawn in May 1964 and stored for preservation as part of the National Collection, being stored at Stratford and then Brighton before moving to the Bluebell Railway, where it is perhaps not the most attractive locomotive, but an important representative of the austerity of wartime construction. No 33037 is seen at Allhallows on 24 September 1960. *F.Hornby*

Right: 'L1' class 4-4-0 No 31786 stands at Tonbridge shed on 23 June 1961, having been cleaned to work a special train. Built as No A786 by the North British Locomotive Co (works No 23367) in April 1926 for the Southern Railway, it was withdrawn in February 1962 and broken up at Eastleigh works. *R.C.Riley*

Below: Stewarts Lane depot always had an excellent reputation for clean locomotives for special occasions. The use of a 73A locomotive on Royal trains to Tattenham Corner for the Derby, and on specials for overseas dignitaries from either Dover or Gatwick to Victoria has been long-standing. The position is unchanged today, the steam locomotives having been replaced by Class 73 electro-diesels, still adorned with a 73A shed plate. Rebuilt 'Battle of Britain' No 34088 *213 Squadron* waits at the depot before moving off to Victoria to take the Royal family to the Derby in May 1963. *Rodney Lissenden*

Above: Out of a class of 40 locomotives, three members of the 'Schools' class have been preserved. No 925 *Cheltenham* is part of the national collection at York, No 926 *Repton* spent nearly 24 years in the USA before returning to Great Britain at the North Yorkshire Moors Railway, and No 928 *Stowe* which spent nearly 10 years at the National Motor Museum, Beaulieu, can now be found on the Bluebell Railway in Sussex. As British Railways No 30928, *Stowe* awaits its next turn of duty at Ashford shed on 28 May 1961. *Rodney Lissenden*

Above: 'K' class 2-6-0 No 32339 stands at Brighton shed on 31 March 1962 about 18 months prior to withdrawal. Robert Billinton introduced this class to the LBSCR in 1913, No 32339 being completed at Brighton works in March 1914 at a cost of £3,150. Most of the work done by the class was on the Central section of the Southern. After 48 years of service No 32339 was taken to Eastleigh for scrapping, having covered nearly a million miles. *Trevor Owen*

Below: The 'L1' class was an improved version of the 'L' class, although not as handsome. There were 15 locomotives in the class, all built by the North British Locomotive Co, and delivered between 1 March and 13 April 1926 at a cost of £5,925 each (works Nos 23356-70) This fine portrait of No 31754 at Stewarts Lane shows the locomotive coaled, ready for its next duty. The final member of the class survived until February 1962, whilst No 31754 was broken up at Eastleigh works after withdrawal in November 1961.
R.C.Riley

Left: R.E.L.Maunsell developed Robert Urie's express passenger 4-6-0 locomotives after their erratic performance, and with a number of modifications to the design, the 'King Arthur' class was constructed by the Southern Railway between 1925 and 1927. The original Urie 'N15' class was built between 1918 and 1923 at Eastleigh works as Nos 736-755. The second batch, Nos 448-457, were built in 1925, also at Eastleigh. Nos 763-792 were built by North British between May and October 1925, and the final batch, Nos 793-806 were constructed at Eastleigh during 1926. A grand total of 74 locomotives. No 30769 *Sir Balan,* one of the North British-built 'Scotch Arthurs', passes St Mary Cray Junction with a Victoria-Ramsgate express on 16 May 1959. *R.C.Riley*

Above: A famous train in the final days of steam in the south-east was the 7.24am (Saturdays only) London Bridge-Ramsgate via Tonbridge, Ashford and Dover, which was much photographed and carefully timed by many enthusiasts. 'D1' class 4-4-0 No 31489 is about to leave Folkestone Junction on 15 May 1960. The locomotive shed on the right used to house the 'R1' 0-6-0Ts for work on the harbour branch. *R.C.Riley*

Above: 'Battle of Britain' class 4-6-2 No 34084 *253 Squadron* emerges from Chelsfield tunnel, Knockholt, with a down Victoria-Dover Marine boat train. The Bulleid Pacifics performed excellent work in Kent, particularly on boat trains which were often loaded to 12 coaches and two vans. The train is within a mile of the summit, after the long climb from Shortlands via Bickley and Petts Wood Junction to Polhill tunnel, then being routed via the South Eastern main line through the Weald of Kent to Dover. This scene was photographed about a year before electrification of the line from Sevenoaks to the coast was completed in 1961. *Derek Cross*

Back cover: 'H' class 0-4-4T No 31322 at Cliffe with the 2.47pm Gravesend Central-Allhallows-on-Sea. *Julian Thompson*